CONTENTS

HAM & CHEESE MORNING QUICHES

PREP: 15 min. \ **TOTAL:** 45 min. \ **MAKES:** 6 servings, 2 quiches each

---

12 slices whole wheat bread

 4 eggs

 4 oz. (½ of 8-oz. tub) *Philadelphia* Neufchâtel Cheese

 1 Tbsp. milk

 ¼ cup finely chopped *Oscar Mayer* Deli Fresh Honey Ham

 2 green onions, sliced

1 **Heat** oven to 400°F.

2 **Use** rolling pin to flatten each bread slice to 5-inch square. Cut out centers with 3½-inch round cookie cutter. Discard trimmings or reserve for another use. Press 1 bread circle onto bottom and up side of each of 12 greased muffin cups.

3 **Bake** 8 to 10 min. or until golden brown. Reduce oven temperature to 350°F. Beat 1 egg and Neufchâtel in medium bowl with wire whisk until well blended. Add remaining 3 eggs, the milk, ham and onions; mix well. Pour into bread cups.

4 **Bake** 18 to 20 min. or until filling in center of each cup is set. Serve warm.

MEDITERRANEAN FRITTATA

PREP: 15 min. \ **TOTAL:** 55 min. \ **MAKES:** 6 servings

---

5 eggs, beaten

4 oz. (½ of 8-oz. tub) *Philadelphia* Neufchâtel Cheese

2 Tbsp. pesto

2 cloves garlic, minced

½ cup *Kraft* Shredded Mozzarella Cheese

1 zucchini, shredded

1 tomato, chopped

3 green onions, sliced

1 Heat oven to 350°F.

2 Mix all ingredients until well blended.

3 Spoon into greased 9-inch pie plate.

4 Bake 40 min. or until center is set. Let stand 5 min. before cutting into wedges to serve.

VARIATION

For a change of pace, substitute *Kraft* Shredded Swiss Cheese for the *Kraft* Shredded Mozzarella Cheese and 1 cup drained, canned stewed tomatoes for the chopped fresh tomato.

SPAGHETTI

PREP: 30 min. \ **TOTAL:** 30 min. \ **MAKES:** 4 servings, 1½ cups each

---

   8 oz. spaghetti, uncooked

   1 lb. extra-lean ground beef

2½ cups spaghetti sauce

   4 oz. (½ of 8-oz. pkg.) *Philadelphia* Neufchâtel Cheese, cubed

   2 Tbsp. *Kraft* Grated Parmesan Cheese

1 **Cook** spaghetti as directed on package, omitting salt.

2 **Meanwhile,** brown meat in large skillet. Stir in sauce and Neufchâtel; cook on low heat 3 to 5 min. or until sauce is well blended and heated through, stirring frequently.

3 **Drain** spaghetti. Add to sauce; mix lightly. Place on platter; top with Parmesan.

SPECIAL EXTRA

Sprinkle with chopped fresh basil or parsley before serving.

CHICKEN-PARMESAN BUNDLES

PREP: 35 min. \ **TOTAL:** 1 hour 5 min. \ **MAKES:** 6 servings

---

> 4 oz. (½ of 8-oz. pkg.) *Philadelphia* Cream Cheese, softened
>
> 1 pkg. (10 oz.) frozen chopped spinach, thawed, well drained
>
> 1¼ cups *Kraft* Shredded Low-Moisture Part-Skim Mozzarella Cheese, divided
>
> 6 Tbsp. *Kraft* Grated Parmesan Cheese, divided
>
> 6 small boneless skinless chicken breast halves (1½ lb.), pounded to ¼-inch thickness
>
> 1 egg
>
> 10 round butter crackers, crushed (about ⅓ cup)
>
> 1½ cups spaghetti sauce

1 **Heat** oven to 375°F.

2 **Mix** cream cheese, spinach, 1 cup mozzarella and 3 Tbsp. Parmesan until well blended; spread onto chicken breasts. Starting at one short end of each breast, roll up chicken tightly. Secure with wooden toothpicks, if desired.

3 **Beat** egg in pie plate. Mix remaining Parmesan and cracker crumbs in separate pie plate. Dip chicken, 1 at a time, in egg, then roll in crumb mixture. Place, seam-sides down, in 13×9-inch baking dish sprayed with cooking spray.

4 **Bake** 30 min. or until chicken is done, heating spaghetti sauce near the end of the chicken baking time. Discard toothpicks. Serve chicken topped with spaghetti sauce and remaining mozzarella.

SPECIAL EXTRA
Sprinkle with chopped fresh basil before serving.

POTATO-TOPPED MINI MEATLOAVES

PREP: 15 min. \ **TOTAL:** 40 min. \ **MAKES:** 6 servings

1 lb. extra-lean ground beef

1 pkg. (6 oz.) *Stove Top* Stuffing Mix

1 cup water

4 oz. (½ of 8-oz. pkg.) *Philadelphia* Cream Cheese, cubed

2 cloves garlic, minced

2 cups hot mashed potatoes

¼ cup chopped fresh parsley

1 jar (12 oz.) beef gravy, warmed

1 Heat oven to 375°F.

2 Mix meat, stuffing mix and water; press into 12 muffin cups sprayed with cooking spray.

3 Bake 20 to 25 min. or until done (160°F).

4 Add cream cheese and garlic to potatoes; stir until cream cheese is melted. Stir in parsley. Scoop over meatloaves. Serve with gravy.

CREAMY MUSTARD CHICKEN

PREP: 30 min. \ **TOTAL:** 30 min. \ **MAKES:** 4 servings

---

  1 tsp. oil

  4 small boneless skinless chicken breast halves (1 lb.)

  ⅓ cup chicken broth

  ¼ cup (¼ of 8-oz. tub) *Philadelphia* **Cream Cheese Spread**

  1 Tbsp. *Grey Poupon* **Harvest Coarse Ground Mustard**

1 Heat oil in large nonstick skillet on medium heat. Add chicken; cook 6 to 8 min. on each side or until done (165°F). Transfer to plate; cover to keep warm.

2 Add broth to skillet; cook on medium heat 3 to 5 min. or until hot. Add cream cheese spread and mustard; cook and stir 2 to 3 min. or until cream cheese is completely melted and sauce is well blended and slightly thickened.

3 Pour sauce over chicken.

SERVING SUGGESTION

Serve with potatoes, hot cooked rice or pasta and your favorite cooked vegetable.

CREAMY BASIL & RED PEPPER PASTA

PREP: 25 min. \ **TOTAL:** 25 min. \ **MAKES:** 4 servings

- **2 cups whole wheat penne pasta, uncooked**
- **1 jar (7 oz.) roasted red peppers, well drained**
- **4 oz. (½ of 8-oz. pkg.) *Philadelphia* Fat Free Cream Cheese, softened**
- **½ cup fat-free milk**
- **½ cup fresh basil**
- **2 Tbsp. *Kraft* Grated Parmesan Cheese**
- **1 lb. boneless skinless chicken breasts, cut into bite-size pieces**

1 Cook pasta as directed on package. Meanwhile, blend all remaining ingredients except chicken in blender until smooth.

2 Spray large skillet with cooking spray. Add chicken; cook on medium-high heat 3 min., stirring frequently. Stir in pepper mixture; simmer on medium heat 5 min. or until heated through, stirring frequently.

3 Drain pasta. Add to chicken mixture; mix lightly.

SPECIAL EXTRA
Garnish with additional fresh basil leaves.

FIESTA CHICKEN ENCHILADAS MADE OVER

PREP: 25 min. \ **TOTAL:** 45 min. \ **MAKES:** 4 servings

---

  1 **lb. boneless skinless chicken breasts, cut into bite-size pieces**

  1 **each large green and red pepper, chopped**

  1 **Tbsp. chili powder**

  ¾ **cup** *Taco Bell*® *Home Originals*® **Thick 'N Chunky Salsa, divided**

  2 **oz. (¼ of 8-oz.-pkg.)** *Philadelphia* **Neufchâtel Cheese, cubed**

  ¾ **cup** *Kraft* **Shredded Cheddar & Monterey Jack Cheeses, divided**

  8 **flour tortillas (8 inch)**

1 Heat oven to 375°F.

2 Heat large heavy nonstick skillet sprayed with cooking spray on medium heat. Add chicken, peppers and chili powder; cook and stir 8 min. or until chicken is done. Stir in ¼ cup salsa and Neufchâtel; cook and stir 3 to 5 min. or until Neufchâtel is melted and mixture is well blended. Stir in ¼ cup shredded cheese.

3 Spoon heaping ⅓ cup chicken mixture down center of each tortilla; roll up. Place, seam-sides down, in 13✕9-inch baking dish sprayed with cooking spray; top with remaining salsa and shredded cheese. Cover.

4 Bake 20 min. or until heated through.

Taco Bell® and *Home Originals*® are trademarks owned and licensed by Taco Bell Corp.

VARIATION
Prepare using corn tortillas. To prevent cracking, warm tortillas as directed on package before using as directed.

ROAST PORK TENDERLOIN SUPPER

PREP: 20 min. \ **TOTAL:** 40 min. \ **MAKES:** 6 servings

---

  2 pork tenderloins (1½ lb.)

  ¼ cup *Grey Poupon* Dijon Mustard

  2 tsp. dried thyme leaves

  1 pkg. (6 oz.) *Stove Top* Stuffing Mix for Chicken

  ½ cup chicken broth

  4 oz. (½ of 8-oz. pkg.) *Philadelphia* Neufchâtel Cheese, cubed

  1 lb. fresh green beans, trimmed, steamed

1 Heat oven to 400°F.

2 Heat large heavy nonstick skillet on medium heat. Add meat; cook 5 min. or until browned on all sides, turning occasionally. Transfer meat to 13×9-inch baking dish, reserving drippings in skillet. Mix mustard and thyme; spread onto meat.

3 Bake 20 min. or until done (145°F). Transfer to carving board; tent with foil. Let stand 5 min. Meanwhile, prepare stuffing as directed on package, reducing margarine to 1 Tbsp.

4 Add broth to same skillet. Bring to boil on high heat. Add Neufchâtel; cook on medium-low heat 2 min. or until Neufchâtel is completely melted and sauce is well blended, stirring constantly.

5 Cut meat into thin slices. Serve topped with sauce along with the stuffing and beans.

NOTE

If you purchased the broth in a 32-oz. pkg., store remaining broth in refrigerator up to 1 week. Or, if you purchased a 14-oz. can, pour the remaining broth into a glass container; store in refrigerator up to 1 week.

ROASTED VEGGIE SANDWICH

PREP: 10 min. \ **TOTAL:** 22 min. \ **MAKES:** 2 servings

- ½ **red pepper**
- 2 **slices red onion (¼ inch thick)**
- 4 **slices <u>each</u> yellow squash and zucchini (¼ inch thick)**
- ⅛ **tsp. black pepper**
- 2 **squares focaccia bread (3 inch), split**
- ¼ **cup (¼ of 8-oz. tub) *Philadelphia* Spinach & Artichoke Cream Cheese Spread**

1 Heat oven to 400°F.

2 Make 2 or 3 small cuts in each short end of red pepper; press pepper to flatten. Place on baking sheet sprayed with cooking spray. Add remaining vegetables. Sprinkle with black pepper.

3 Bake 10 to 12 min. or until crisp-tender.

4 Spread cut sides of focaccia with cream cheese spread; fill with vegetables.

USE YOUR GRILL

Place grill pan on grill; heat on medium heat. Add vegetables to heated pan; brush with 1 Tbsp. olive oil. Grill 10 min. or until crisp-tender, turning after 5 min.

THREE-CHEESE CHICKEN PENNE PASTA BAKE

PREP: 25 min. \ **TOTAL:** 45 min. \ **MAKES:** 4 servings, 2 cups each

---

1½ **cups multi-grain penne pasta, uncooked**

1 **pkg. (9 oz.) fresh baby spinach leaves**

1 **lb. boneless skinless chicken breasts, cut into bite-size pieces**

1 **tsp. dried basil leaves**

1 **can (14½ oz.) diced tomatoes, drained**

1 **jar (14 oz.) spaghetti sauce**

2 **oz. (¼ of 8-oz. pkg.) *Philadelphia* Neufchâtel Cheese, cubed**

1 **cup *Kraft* 2% Milk Shredded Mozzarella Cheese, divided**

2 **Tbsp. *Kraft* Grated Parmesan Cheese**

1 **Heat** oven to 375°F.

2 **Cook** pasta in large saucepan as directed on package, omitting salt and adding spinach to the boiling water for last minute.

3 **Meanwhile,** heat large nonstick skillet sprayed with cooking spray on medium-high heat. Add chicken and basil; cook 3 min. or until chicken is no longer pink, stirring frequently. Stir in tomatoes and spaghetti sauce; bring to boil. Reduce heat to low; simmer 3 min. or until chicken is done. Add Neufchâtel; cook and stir until melted.

4 **Drain** pasta and spinach; return to same saucepan. Add chicken mixture; mix lightly. Stir in ½ cup mozzarella cheese. Spoon into 2-qt. or 8-inch square baking dish.

5 **Bake** 20 min. or until heated through. Sprinkle with remaining mozzarella and Parmesan cheeses. Bake 3 min. or until mozzarella is melted.

CREAMY POTATO-LEEK SOUP

PREP: 20 min. \ **TOTAL:** 1 hour \ **MAKES:** 10 servings, 1 cup each

---

- **2 leeks, white and light green parts cut into 1-inch pieces**
- **2 lb. Yukon Gold potatoes (about 8), peeled, cut into ½-inch cubes**
- **2 Tbsp. *Kraft* Tuscan House Italian Dressing**
- **1 Tbsp. chopped fresh rosemary**
- **3 cups water**
- **1 can (14½ oz.) chicken broth**
- **1 pkg. (8 oz.) *Philadelphia* Cream Cheese, cubed, divided**

1 Heat oven to 400°F.

2 Combine vegetables, dressing and rosemary; spread onto baking sheet. Bake 35 to 40 min. or until vegetables are tender and golden brown, stirring occasionally.

3 Place water, broth and ¾ cup cream cheese cubes in large saucepan; cook on medium heat 3 min. or until mixture is well blended, stirring frequently with whisk. Stir in vegetables.

4 Blend soup, in batches, in blender until smooth. Return to saucepan; bring to boil. Thin soup with additional water, if desired. Serve topped with remaining cream cheese cubes.

SPECIAL EXTRA

Top with additional chopped fresh rosemary just before serving.

CREAMY ROSÉ PENNE

PREP: 20 min. \ **TOTAL:** 20 min. \ **MAKES:** 4 servings, 1¼ cups each

---

   3 **cups penne pasta, uncooked**

1½ **cups spaghetti sauce**

   ⅓ **cup (⅓ of 8-oz. tub)** *Philadelphia* **Cream Cheese Spread**

   ¼ **cup fresh basil**

1 **Cook** pasta as directed on package, omitting salt.

2 **Meanwhile,** heat spaghetti sauce in nonstick skillet on medium-high heat. Stir in cream cheese spread; cook and stir 2 to 3 min. or until melted.

3 **Drain** pasta; toss with sauce until evenly coated. Top with basil.

20-MINUTE SKILLET SALMON

PREP: 20 min. \ **TOTAL:** 20 min. \ **MAKES:** 4 servings

- **2 Tbsp. oil**
- **4 skin-on salmon fillets (1 lb.)**
- **1 cup fat-free milk**
- **½ cup (½ of 8-oz. tub)** *Philadelphia* **Neufchâtel Cheese**
- **½ cup chopped cucumbers**
- **2 Tbsp. chopped fresh dill**

1 Heat oil in large skillet on medium-high heat. Add fish; cook 5 min. on each side or until fish flakes easily with fork. Remove from skillet; cover to keep warm.

2 Add milk and Neufchâtel to skillet; cook and stir until cream cheese is melted and mixture is well blended. Stir in cucumbers and dill.

3 Return fish to skillet; cook 2 min. or until heated through. Serve topped with cream cheese sauce.

SPECIAL EXTRA
Garnish salmon with fresh dill sprigs before serving.